For my two greatest treasures (A.S.)
For Jann – lifesaver, colorist and treasure trove, all rolled into one! (J.T.)

Published in the German language originally under the title: Der Größte Schatz der Welt
© 2016 Ravensburger Verlag GmbH, Ravensburg, Germany.
ISBN 978-3-473-44674-2
Written by Andrea Schütze.
Illustrated by Joëlle Tourlonias.

All rights reserved. No part of this book may be reproduced in any form without
written permission from the publisher.

Copyright of the English edition by Evergreen Books.
Evergreen Books is an imprint of:
Freude am Buch GmbH, Robert-Bosch-Straße 32 A, 63303 Dreieich, Germany.
English language translation copyright © Rachel Ward, 2021.

ISBN 978-3-96326-003-2
Printed in Canada.

www.evergreen-books.de

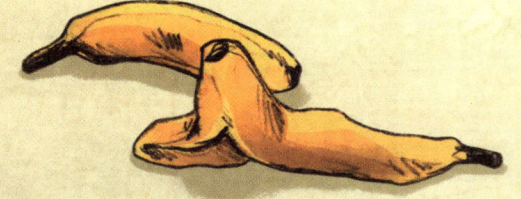

THE World's Greatest TREASURE

Written by Andrea Schütze
Illustrated by Joëlle Tourlonias

It's the afternoon. Momo the little monkey is bored. Very bored.

"Booor-riiiing!" moans Momo.

"Go and get me some berries, my treasure!" Mommy Monkey calls.

What did mommy say? It sounded like: "Go and get me some buried treasure!"

Don't forget how noisy it is in the jungle... It's hardly surprising that the little monkey misheard what mommy said.

A treasure hunt! What a great idea! Mommy deserves the most precious treasure in all the world, thinks Momo. Gold, silver, diamonds, precious stones...!

Everyone knows a treasure hunt is hard work.
You need a big shovel, a sharp pickax, a sack for all the gold and coins and, above all, a treasure map.
Where's Momo supposed to get all that from?
The little monkey sits down on a rock for a good, long think.

"Yew neely sat on me," says a sharp-tongued voice.

"Oh, Whiptongue Frog, I'm sorry!" says the little monkey. "What are yew dooing here anyhew?" asks the frog.

"I'm looking for treasure. You know, gold and silver, jewels and diamonds. Do you want to join me?" asks Momo.

"Noo, noo, I'm purfuctly happee. Mewsic is my treasuure! Mewsic does you go-ood! I'm givin' a whistlin' concurt in juhst a minutt," answers the frog, who hops away, humming.

Momo decides to head to the village and ask around there.

"Hey, Chameleon," Momo exclaims. "Great disguise!"

"I'm advertising my shop," says the chameleon proudly. "What are you up to, young monkey?"

"I'm looking for treasure. You know, gold and silver, jewels and diamonds. Can you help me?"

"No," says the chameleon, "I've already got a treasure: my disguises! The jungle is a dangerous place. You need to be able to make yourself invisible, buddy."

"Aye, aye, sir!" says the little monkey, and he hops on.

"Hello, Snake. I'm hunting the greatest treasure in the world. Gold, silver, pearls, jewels, you know! Can you help me?"

"Ss-s-certainly not," hisses the snake. "I'm all the treas-s-s-sure I need mys-s-self. I can twis-s-t my body to s-s-spell all the letters-s-s of the alphabet."

Momo walks on with a sigh.

"Won't you s-s-s-stay a while? I could danc-s-s-s-e your name!" whispers the snake.

But Momo's promised to bring his mommy a buried treasure!

At the little theater, the parrot is strutting up and down the stage.

Momo says: "Excuse me please, Mr. Doodle, I'm looking for the most precious treasure in the whole world. Could you help me?"

"Don't bother me with such childish nonsense," answers the parrot, ruffling up his magnificent plumage. "Didn't you hear my voice? That is my treasure. It means I can be whatever I like!"

The parrot points to the snake. "Anything els-s-s-e is-s-s-s a pure was-s-s-s-te of time."

Momo hops on with a giggle.

THIS EVENING, COME AND SEE
THE Great Flap Doodle
The World's Best Impressionist

It's really hard to track down the world's greatest treasure. Everyone seems to have one already. But nobody has any precious stones or anything like that! The little monkey is rather puzzled. Momo stops by the spider's market stall.

"Come and buy! Freshly caught inshectsh! Tashty and good for the digeshtion! Cheap, nutrishioush and delishioush!" the spider calls out.

"Hello, Mrs. Spider, I'm looking for a precious treasure. Could you give me a clue?" the little monkey asks.

"Yesh," says the spider cheerfully. "Shee here, little monkey, the world'sh mosht preshioush treasure."

The spider points at her splendid web.

"But I tell you what, you go and ashk the shloth. He'sh got all day jusht to hang around, thinking!"

TODAY'S SPECIAL: Fresh Insects

The sloth seems to be sleeping. The little monkey coughs.

The sloth opens an eye and mumbles: "Hey, how's it hanging, dude?"

"Um," Momo says shyly. "I'd like to find the greatest treasure in the world. Diamonds, gold and stuff. Could you help me maybe?"

"That's what I call a plan!" yawns the sloth. "No problemo. I've got it!"

"Really?" exclaims the little monkey eagerly. "Where is it exactly?"

"In my dreams, kid," mumbles the sleepy sloth. "In my dreams I can have everything I want. You should try it, dreaming."

And just like that, the sloth is asleep again.

What now? The sun will be setting soon, and the little monkey hasn't even found the teeniest, tiniest diamond.

All of a sudden, Momo hears a deep voice whispering: "I hear you're looking for the world's greatest treasure?"

It's Dingo, a wise, old dog. He owns nothing but his old barrel, and he does nothing at all, apart from simply being.

"Yes," answers Momo reverently. "Jewels, gold, stuff like that…"

"Uh-huh, I see," sighs Dingo. "Yes, well, then go home and listen to your mother when she takes you in her arms. You'll learn more about treasure than you can ever imagine!"

The little monkey gives a shy nod.

Dingo cocks his head towards the sky: "Hurry yourself, monkey child, it'll be dark soon."

The little monkey sets gloomily off for home. And all at once, Momo is standing alone in the dark jungle, starting to feel scared.
But, fortunately, just then a firefly taxi flies past.

"Pretty late for such a little monkey!" buzzes the firefly. "Come on, I'll take you home."

"Oh, I was on a treasure hunt..." Momo replies.

"I see! Total flop, was it?" asks the firefly.

"Nobody wanted to help me because everyone had a treasure already. Now, don't you say you've got one too!"

"But I do! You're walking right behind it," answers the firefly, proudly waggling his glowing bottom. "The very finest of taillights!"

Momo feels sad. But he can already see a glimmering through the dense trees. And then he hears his mommy, calling for him anxiously.

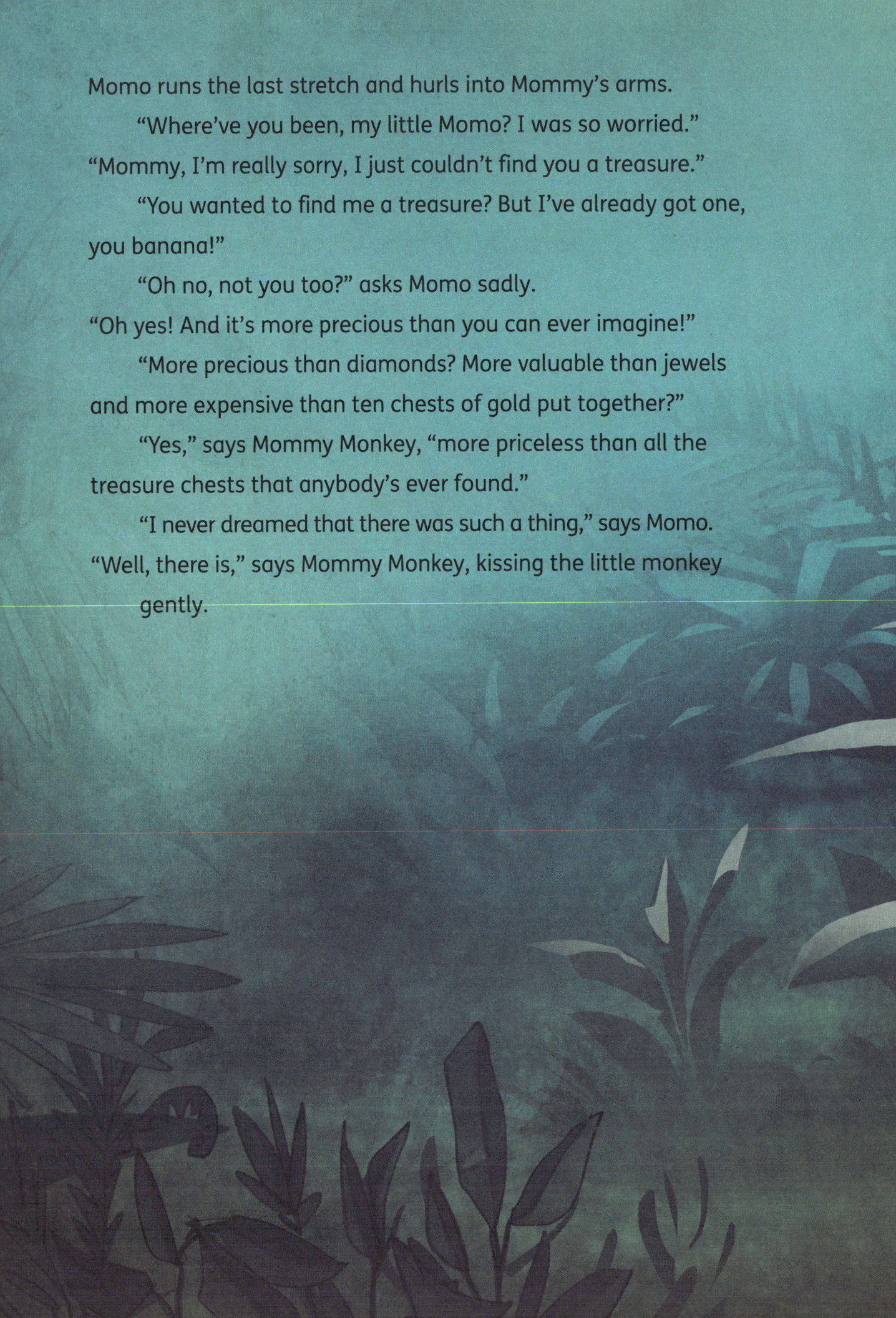

Momo runs the last stretch and hurls into Mommy's arms.

"Where've you been, my little Momo? I was so worried."
"Mommy, I'm really sorry, I just couldn't find you a treasure."
"You wanted to find me a treasure? But I've already got one, you banana!"
"Oh no, not you too?" asks Momo sadly.
"Oh yes! And it's more precious than you can ever imagine!"
"More precious than diamonds? More valuable than jewels and more expensive than ten chests of gold put together?"
"Yes," says Mommy Monkey, "more priceless than all the treasure chests that anybody's ever found."
"I never dreamed that there was such a thing," says Momo.
"Well, there is," says Mommy Monkey, kissing the little monkey gently.

"You must take very good care of it then!" says the little monkey.

"Yes! I do. Every minute of the day. Even so, I thought I'd lost it today," says Mommy Monkey.

"I can't believe you have a thing like that," Momo gasps.
"Every mommy does."

"Every mommy?"
"Every mommy!"

"But a treasure like that can't be so special?" asks Momo.
"Of course it is! Every single one is unique and irreplaceable!"

"Can I see?" Momo pesters.
Mommy Monkey gives Momo a mirror to hold.

The little monkey's getting impatient: "Where is it then? Where's the world's greatest treasure?"

"Look in the mirror and you'll see!" says Mommy Monkey tenderly.
The little monkey looks in the mirror. And looks. And looks.

And slowly Momo starts to understand all kinds of things…

So there, you see:
sometimes you go looking for a treasure and end up
finding yourself. Isn't that nice?

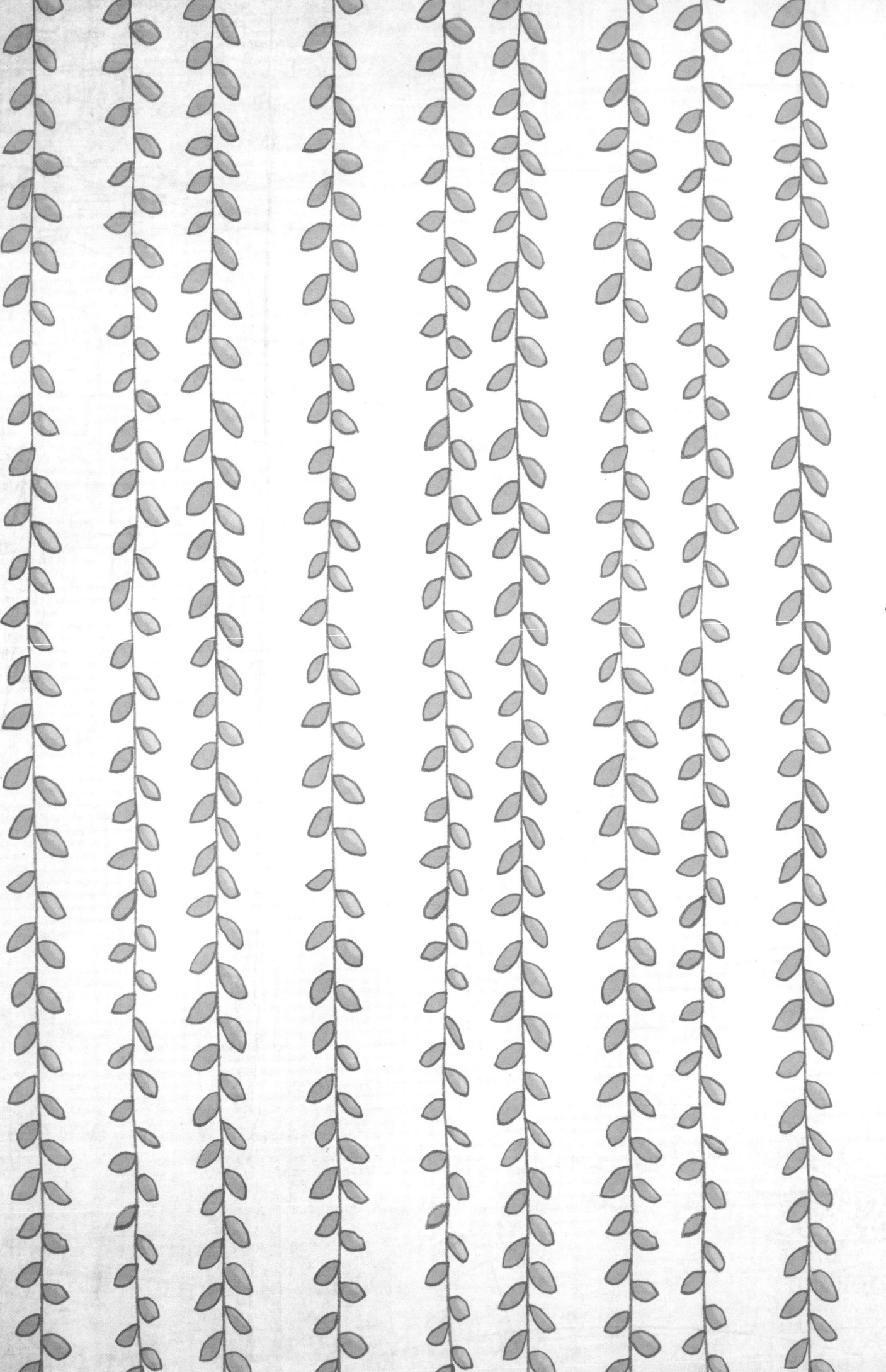